You're One in a Million

by

R. W. Schambach

POWER PUBLICATIONS • TYLER, TEXAS

You're One in a Million

SCHAMBACH REVIVALS, INC.
P. O. BOX 9009
TYLER, TX 75711-9009

ISBN 1-888361-12-3

CONTENTS

YOU'RE ONE IN A MILLION!

Do you know how special you are? God loves you so much, He kept leaning on you with His love until you surrendered your life to Him.

When you said, "Yes," to Jesus — you became a member of God's family. You are His child; you now belong to Him.

Being a child of God is a great privilege. In so many ways, God has provided for you. This book will help you understand what God has already done for you through His Son, Jesus.

He gave everything to help you succeed.

God also has a job for you to do. He wants you to represent Him on this earth. You are to be His ambassador. That means the way you live your life is very important.

This book will help you understand how to grow in your understanding of God and your personal relationship with Him.

Read it carefully. Do as I instruct you; I know <u>you will make it</u> as God's child. I am praying for you.

Allow me to be the first to welcome you to God's family. You are my relative. Remember God thinks you are special.

Recently, He laid it on my heart to win one million souls to Jesus. I am so excited that you are **one in a million!**

Your Power Preacher,

R. W. Schambach

Chapter One

YOU ARE WORTH A LOT TO GOD

"What do you think? If a man has a hundred sheep, and one of them goes astray, does he not leave the ninety-nine and go to the mountains to seek the one that is straying?

"And if he should find it, assuredly, I say to you, he rejoices more over that sheep than over the ninety-nine that did not go astray.

"Even so it is not the will of your Father who is in heaven that one of these little ones should perish."
(Matthew 18:12,13,14)

God is rejoicing over you right now. Jesus said He doesn't want <u>one</u> person to perish.

Since you asked Jesus into your heart and believed on Him — you now have eternal life:

"For God so loved the world, that he gave his only begotten Son, that whosoever believeth in him should not perish, but have everlasting life."
(John 3:16 KJV)

I want you to think about how much God loves you. He saw you as a lost sheep. You were away from the fold, outside of God's family. Yet, you were worth a lot to God. He had people praying for you. He sent a preacher to you. He kept working on you until you surrendered.

The best thing He did was to send Jesus, His Son, to die on a Roman cross for you. Historically, it was a bloody and gruesome death reserved for the worst convicts. Christ's own people rejected Him as a liar or a crazy person. Jesus died a lonely, painful death — He suffered greatly so that you could be part of God's family.

"But God demonstrates His own love toward us, in that while we were still sinners, Christ died for us."
(Romans 5:8)

Think about it. Even when you were in your sin, doing things that God hates — He saw something of value in you. He saw something worth saving. He didn't want to throw you away, but clean you up and make you a brand new person.

I want you to get this point — you are very special. Open your Bible to Luke's Gospel, Chapter 15. In this chapter, Jesus tells the religious leaders about God's love for sinners. He compares the sinner to a lost sheep, a valuable lost coin, and a runaway, prodigal son who is out of relationship with his father.

In each case, great rejoicing takes place when that which was lost is found again. Oh, hallelujah! God gets excited when one of His lost ones is found! In fact, angels in heaven are throwing a party because someone of great value has been found — that's you!

Sometimes the devil talks to you and wants you to think that you are bad or worthless or that God doesn't love you. When you start thinking like that, get your Bible out and remember what God has said about you. You are <u>valuable</u>.

> *"I will praise You, for I am fearfully and wonderfully made...How precious also are Your thoughts to me, O God! How great is the sum of them."*
> (Psalm 139:14a;17)

Chapter Two

GOD WANTS TO BE YOUR FRIEND

"Greater love has no one than this, than to lay down one's life for his friends. You are My friends if you do whatever I command you."
(John 15:13,14)

When you gave your life to Jesus, you became a Christian, or a Christ-follower. You didn't "change religions," but you entered a relationship with the God of the universe. You can talk to God as a heavenly Father; God will also talk to you. You began the most beautiful relationship in the world — you are a friend of God.

Your friendship with God will grow when you learn the way He thinks and live the way He wants you to live. The first thing you will learn about God is His holiness. He cannot live with sin. Sin is the enemy of God. That is why He wants you to learn His ways, so you can stay in close fellowship with Him.

Hear these words of Jesus:

"If anyone loves Me, he will keep My word; and My Father will love him, and We will come to him and make Our home with him."
(John 14:23)

When you accept Jesus into your heart and determine to live for Him, both the Father and the Son will make a home in your heart. In fact, Jesus is described as the "friend who sticks closer than a brother." He will be the best Friend you ever had. You can talk to Him at any time of the day or night. He will never leave nor forsake you.

God lives in your heart through the Holy Spirit. When you accepted Jesus into your heart, He entered by means of the Holy Spirit who is also known as the Holy Ghost. Just before Jesus died, He told His disciples about the Holy Spirit:

"Nevertheless I tell you the truth. It is to your advantage that I go away; for if I do not go away, the Helper will not come to you; but if I depart, I will send Him to you...

However, when He, the Spirit of truth, has come, He will guide you into all truth..."
(John 16:7,13a)

The Holy Spirit lives inside of you — in your heart. He talks to you, telling you what Jesus likes and what He hates. He will help you live right and be God's friend.

Just think about how good and amazing God's love is. He wanted to be our Friend so much, He created us in such a way that He can live, by His Spirit, inside of us. That tells me He wanted to be involved in every area of our lives. He wanted <u>close</u> fellowship.

As you grow in your friendship with God, you will grow disappointed in yourself at times. You will see that your heart is still tempted to sin. The Holy Spirit will let you know in your heart when you are about to make a wrong decision. He will convict you when you commit a sin.

Because God doesn't want to lose you as a friend, He provided a way for you to stay in close fellowship with Him. Learn this great principle now, so you can walk close to Jesus every day:

> *"If we say that we have no sin, we deceive ourselves, and the truth is not in us.*
>
> *If we confess our sins, He is faithful and just to forgive us our sins and to cleanse us from all unrighteousness."*
> (1 John 1:8,9)

When you sin, pray right away and ask God to forgive you. Tell Him you are sorry for breaking His trust and you need His help so you won't sin in the same way again. Make this a daily practice before you lay your head down to sleep. In this way, you will continue to walk as God's friend.

Don't forget how special you are. God the Father, Son and Holy Ghost live in you. God will be your best friend — He is always listening for your call. When you read the Bible and pray daily, He will tell you what is right and what is wrong. By His Spirit, He will help you live holy.

Chapter Three

GOD HAS ADOPTED YOU

"But when the fullness of the time had come, God sent forth His Son, born of a woman, born under the law,

to redeem those who were under the law, that we might receive the adoption as sons.

And because you are sons, God has sent forth the Spirit of His Son into your hearts, crying out, 'Abba, Father!'

Therefore you are no longer a slave but a son, and if a son, then an heir of God through Christ."
(Galatians 4:4-7)

The more you read the Bible, the more you will discover

how much God loves you, and how great a salvation He has given you. You are so special to God, He designed a plan of redemption that would allow you to be <u>more than a friend</u> — He wanted you as part of His family.

When Jesus walked and talked on this earth, He often referred to God as His Father — His heavenly Father. His words pictured God as an intimately involved person. When Jesus was in need, He talked to His Father. Before Jesus went to the next place of ministry, He talked to His Father. Jesus taught us to pray to the Father for every need to be met.

Because Jesus died on the cross and became a sacrifice for our sins, there is no longer a barrier of sin between you and God. This is what Jesus had in mind all along. He wanted you to call God "Father" too.

When the Bible says, "God has sent forth the Spirit of His Son into your hearts, crying out, 'Abba, Father,'" it refers to the fact that your life in Jesus has brought you into a new and wonderful relationship with God. You can call God "Daddy."

Many people today need a heavenly Father. Sometimes earthly fathers show God's love to their children; but often, earthly fathers are too busy for their kids — some aren't even home. Worse yet, some fathers are abusive with their children. This is not the kind of Father Jesus introduced you to.

Your heavenly Father has adopted you. He will feed you, clothe you, listen to you, instruct you, correct you and protect you. You have all the rights and privileges of a "son" or "daughter." Just as the verse says, you are "an heir of God through Christ." (Galatians 4:7b) Jesus taught about the care of the Heavenly Father:

> *"Look at the birds of the air, for they neither sow nor reap nor gather into barns; yet your heavenly Father feeds them. Are you not of more value than they?...*

18

So why do you worry about clothing? Consider the lilies of the field, how they grow: they neither toil nor spin;

and yet I say to you that even Solomon in all his glory was not arrayed like one of these.

Now if God so clothes the grass of the field, which today is, and tomorrow is thrown into the oven, will He not much more clothe you, O you of little faith?

Therefore do not worry, saying, 'What shall we eat?' or 'What shall we drink?' or 'What shall we wear?...'

For your heavenly Father knows that you need all these things.

But seek first the kingdom of God and His righteousness, and all these things shall be added to you."
(Matthew 6:26,28-31,32b,33)

Oh, praise God! I hope you are getting excited. God truly will supply all of your needs — He deeply cares for you. You are not alone, and you are not forgotten.

Most of us love going to our Mama's house or apartment. That is where we feel most at home. We will put our feet up on Mama's coffee table; we will walk right into Mama's kitchen, open the refrigerator and take anything we want. We don't ask Mom for a drink of water — we help ourselves. Why? Because we belong to her. She knows us — we know her.

That's the way it is with God. He wants us to feel at home

with Him. We have access to all that belongs to Him, because Jesus made us part of the family.

> *"And He* [Jesus] *came and preached peace to you who were afar off and to those who were near.*
>
> *For through Him we both have access by one Spirit to the Father.*
>
> *Now, therefore, you are no longer strangers and foreigners, but fellow citizens with the saints and members of the household of God."*
> (Ephesians 2:17-19)

Chapter Four

A BRAND NEW YOU!

"Therefore, if anyone is in Christ, he is a new creation; old things have passed away; behold, all things have become new."
(2 Corinthians 5:17)

"Let him who stole steal no longer, but rather let him labor, working with his hands what is good, that he may have something to give him who has need."
(Ephesians 4:28)

When you asked Jesus to come live in your heart, something changed. The Bible says that you became a new person — all the old things have passed away; everything has become new.

You used to be a sinner; now you are a saint through Jesus

Christ. You used to be an enemy to God; now you are His friend — through Jesus Christ. Once you were on your way to Hell; now you will live forever with God in Heaven — because of what Jesus did for you on the cross.

"How did I change?" you may ask. "I don't look different. I have the same body. Yet, in my heart I know I'm different. I'm softer and I feel as though chains have broken off my heart. It's as though I feel really alive for the first time."

You are describing the work of salvation. When you believed on Jesus in faith, you were saved from sin. You didn't have to earn it or work for it — He did it!

> *"For by grace you have been saved through faith, and that not of yourselves; it is the gift of God, not of works, lest anyone should boast."*
> (Ephesians 2:8,9)

Your sins once made you "dead" to God. You had no spiritual life because of your separation from God. Yet, *"...you He made alive, who were dead in trespasses and sins."* (Ephesians 2:1)

Even though your heart is brand new and freed from the bondage of sin, you must learn to live your life God's way now. The only way you can learn is to read the Bible and ask God to show you the way to change.

The Bible talks about making a conscious effort to put away the old life:

> *"But now you yourselves are to put off all these: anger, wrath, malice, blasphemy, filthy language out of your mouth. Do not lie to one another, since you have put off the old man with his deeds,*
>
> *and have put on the new man...*

Therefore, as the elect of God, holy and beloved, put on tender mercies, kindness, humility, meekness, longsuffering..."
(Colossians 3:8-9,10a,12)

Every new Christian has a lot to learn. It is very important to read the Bible every day. Some people read it when they get up in the morning and before they go to bed. Others make a special quiet time each day to read the Bible. However you choose, make time each day to read God's Word and find out how He wants you to change.

When you start reading the Bible, you may get a little discouraged. You will see so many areas that will need change in your life. You will feel that the job is too difficult.

That is why you must also pray every day. Ask God to help you change areas of your life. Ask Him for self-control. Thank Him for saving you and making you a new creation. Your daily communion with God will give you strength to keep on growing as a righteous person.

Jesus gave a pattern for praying in Matthew 6:9 (). He said,

"In this manner, therefore, pray:

"Our Father in heaven, [remember you are in God's family]
"Hallowed be Your name [worship God — tell Him He is worthy of praise]
"Your kingdom come. Your will be done on earth as it is in heaven [realize that all your desires must be placed in submission to His will]
"Give us this day our daily bread. [ask God for your needs to be met]
"And forgive us our debts, as we forgive our debtors. [remember to daily ask forgiveness of sins]

"And do not lead us into temptation, but deliver us from the evil one. [ask God to help you live holy, and keep you from the evil one]
"For Yours is the kingdom and the power and the glory forever. Amen." [End your prayer with worship]

You are a brand new creation. Everything is changed — you are even eating brand new food. You used to take in all kinds of movies and television programs. That is junk food and it makes you spiritually sick. Now you are feeding on the Word of God — the Bible. It will help you grow up strong and stable as a Christian.

When you read the Bible and pray every day, you will begin to succeed in life as never before. God makes your way to prosper.

"Blessed is the man who walks not in the counsel of the ungodly, nor stands in the path of sinners, nor sits in the seat of the scornful; But his delight is in the law of the Lord and in His law he meditates day and night.

"He shall be like a tree planted by the rivers of water, That brings forth its fruit in its season, Whose leaf also shall not wither; And whatsoever he does shall prosper."
(Psalm 1:1-3)

Take time to read the Bible and pray. Study the word and hide it in your heart. Allow the Holy Spirit to help you change according to the Word of God. When you do, your life will begin to change and you will begin to prosper in ways you never believed possible.

Do not become discouraged if the changes are slow.

Remember, you are already a new creature in Christ because of salvation. As you remain faithful in praying and reading the Bible, soon others will begin to notice a brand new you!

Chapter Five

WELCOME TO THE FAMILY!

I am thrilled to be the first to welcome you to the family of God! Whether you like it or not, you are my relative; I am your brother. We are related through the bloodline — through the precious blood of Jesus Christ that was shed on the cross of Calvary:

> *"knowing that you were not redeemed with corruptible things, like silver or gold...but with the precious blood of Christ, as of a lamb without blemish and without spot."*
> (1 Peter 1:18a,19)

You may not be aware of it, but God has chosen you before the beginning of the world to be part of His family. He intended His earthly family to represent Him on this earth. God chose you and me so that our lives could show the truth of His love to others.

One thing that convinces people that Jesus is alive is the beautiful love they have for others.

> ***"Since you have purified your souls in obeying the truth through the Spirit in sincere love of the brethren, love one another fervently with a pure heart, having been born again..."***
> (1 Peter 1:22,23a)

Jesus gave a name to this family. He called it the Church. The word *"church"* comes from a Greek word that means *"called out ones."* You and I have been called out of the world, called out of our sin, and called out of bondage to the devil. Aren't you glad that God called you out?

One of the purposes of the Church is to worship God. The Church comes together as a family to praise God and thank Him for calling them out of bondage:

> ***"you also, as living stones, are being built up a spiritual house, a holy priesthood, to offer up spiritual sacrifices acceptable to God through Jesus Christ."***
> (1 Peter 2:5)

> ***"...I will declare Your name to My brethren; In the midst of the assembly I will sing praise to You."***
> (Hebrews 2:12b)

Another purpose of the Church is to instruct new believers in the Word of God. God appointed pastors and teachers to govern the Church and to teach His people the truth so that they could grow stronger.

> ***"And He Himself*** [Jesus] ***gave some to be apostles, some prophets, some evangelists, and some pastors***

and teachers,

"for the equipping of the saints for the work of the ministry, for the edifying of the body of Christ...

"that we should no longer be children, tossed to and fro and carried about with every wind of doctrine, by the trickery of men, in the cunning craftiness of deceitful plotting."
(Ephesians 4:11,12,14)

Beloved friend, one of the first things you must do as a child of God is find a church home. You will have many to visit — many to pray about. Yet this one thing I know, if you earnestly seek God about placing you with a good church, He will lead you to just the right one. He wants you to be in church more than you want to be there.

"And let us consider one another in order to stir up love and good works, not forsaking the assembling of ourselves together, as is the manner of some, but exhorting one another, and so much the more as you see the Day approaching."
(Hebrews 10:24,25)

The following is a list of things to consider in finding a church home:

1.   Does the church have a pastor who preaches the Bible as the only authority for your life?

2.   Does the church have Bible classes where I can be taught regularly? Are there classes for my children?

3.   Does the congregation have a free worship of God? Are people willing to raise their hands in worship to God?

4.   Does the pastor encourage each believer to win souls and pray for missions?

5.   Does the pastor encourage the congregation to seek the Baptism of the Holy Ghost and the gifts of the Holy Spirit?

6.   Does this church welcome anyone to worship with them, regardless of race or social status?

7.   Is this a church I would enjoy attending weekly, and could make a part of my regular schedule?

8.   Is God impressing me that this is the right church?

Keep in mind, there are no perfect people and no perfect churches. If you find a church that has a lot of the important things a church should have, keep attending until God indicates a change. Do not base your attendance on how people treat you, or if you feel comfortable. Most new experiences take some time getting used to. But when you are faithful, God will place you in a church that feels like "home."

Once you have found that church, attend it faithfully. Pay your tithes there. Be at every possible service. Be active in the work of the Lord. You will grow stronger each week. If you have questions or a problem, go to the pastor. He will help you in your new walk with God.

A third purpose for the Church is to win souls to Jesus Christ. Once you have learned and have grown, God will begin to use you in evangelism. Sometimes churches will have outreach programs to the inner city. Others will take mission teams to other countries. Find a place where you can be active in the Lord's work.

Let me be honest. The enemy of your soul does not want you to succeed. He will put every excuse in your head to stay away from church. Recognize who is talking to your mind. The enemy does not want you to grow in faith. He does not want you to be a soul winner. Don't be afraid when he tries to discourage you. Jesus spoke with great confidence about the church.

> *"...and on this rock I will build My church, and the gates of Hades shall not prevail against it.*
>
> *"And I will give you the keys of the kingdom of heaven, and whatever you bind on earth will be bound in heaven, and whatever you loose on earth will be loosed in heaven."*
> (Matthew 16:18,19)

Welcome to the family!

Chapter Six

HE GIVES YOU THE POWER!

One of the first things a new Christian learns is how easy it is to go back to old habits. Even though you have been freed from the curse and bondage of sin, your old nature will still show its ugly head from time to time.

You may be tempted to sin; or the devil may plague you with guilt over the past. Some Christians are fearful of telling others about Jesus, because they are afraid they will do some terrible thing that will bring dishonor to Christ.

You will soon realize that you cannot live this Christian life in your own strength. You will need a power that comes from God living in you. Jesus promised His disciples power. He told them when the Holy Spirit came "upon" them, they would receive power.

At the time you accepted Jesus, the Holy Spirit entered your heart. He lives with you at all times. The Bible speaks of a power that the Holy Spirit gives for service, that is an experience called **the baptism in the Holy Spirit**.

John the Baptist spoke about this kind of baptism:

*"I indeed baptize you with water unto repentance,
but He who is coming after me is mightier than I,
whose sandals I am not worthy to carry. He will
baptize you with the Holy Spirit and fire."*
(Matthew 3:11)

When John speaks of Jesus baptizing with the Holy Spirit
and fire, he is referring to the cleansing work of the Holy Ghost.
When you pray to receive the baptism of the Holy Ghost, He will
be released in a more powerful way to help you live holy before
God.

Jesus told His disciples about another important gift that
comes with the baptism of the Holy Ghost — **power**:

*"But you shall receive power when the Holy Spirit
has come upon you; and you shall be witnesses to
Me in Jerusalem, and in all Judea and Samaria,
and to the end of the earth."*
(Acts 1:8)

This is the secret to our Christian walk. When you pray,
ask God to pour out His Spirit upon you in full measure. Tell Him
you want to be immersed in the Holy Ghost. You want to have the
power to lead others to Christ — to be a bold witness.

When the disciples were baptized in the Holy Ghost, they
knew it! God gave them an outward sign that something
spectacular had happened on the inside:

*"And they were all filled with the Holy Spirit and
began to speak with other tongues, as the Spirit
gave them utterance."*
(Acts 2:4)

As the disciples prayed in full openness to God, the Holy
Spirit spoke through them miraculously. They knew they had

received the promise of the Father. You will know that you have been baptized in the Holy Spirit when you speak in tongues.

Later on in the book of Acts, when Paul took a missionary journey, he found some believers who had not heard of the baptism of the Holy Ghost. Paul knew they needed it right away.

> *"And when Paul had laid hands on them, the Holy Spirit came upon them, and they spoke with tongues and prophesied."*
> (Acts 19:6)

Some people believe that this experience does not exist for the believer today. They will teach that you do not need it. Some may even say it is of the devil. Do not believe what man says to you; base what you believe on the Bible.

Consider what Peter said when he received the baptism of the Holy Spirit:

> *"Then Peter said to them, 'Repent, and let every one of you be baptized in the name of Jesus Christ for the remission of sins; and you shall receive the gift of the Holy Spirit.*
>
> *"'For the promise is to you and to your children, and to all who are afar off, as many as the Lord our God will call.'"*
> (Acts 2:38,39)

If you pray once and do not have the experience of speaking in tongues, should you give up? No! Sometimes we must pray earnestly for a while, blocking out all distractions. Often, the baptism of the Holy Ghost comes when a person opens their heart to God and begins to worship the Lord. You can receive the baptism in your living room — God will baptize you in the Holy

Ghost.

> ***"If you then, being evil, know how to give good
> gifts to your children, how much more will your
> heavenly Father give the Holy Spirit to those who
> ask Him!"***
> (Luke 11:13)

Remember, you are going to need a reservoir of power to
live for God and be His witness on a daily basis. Pray every day
to receive the baptism — then pray every day in the Holy Spirit.
This is how you are strengthened on the inside:

> ***"But you, beloved, building yourselves up on your
> most holy faith, praying in the Holy Spirit..."***
> (Jude 20)

Oh, hallelujah! God has given us a great salvation. He
looked on you and me and saw something of value. He paid a
great price to save us — and He adopted us into His family. God
loved us so much that He was willing to give all that He had to see
you and me succeed. The wonder is, He saw our full potential —
He knew we could be used to win others to Jesus. God believes in
you — He believes in me.

It may seem that we have a great task ahead of us; we do.
Yet, be encouraged. When God gives you a job description, He
also gives you the power to accomplish that job. Before you
undertake anything for the Lord — be baptized in the Holy Ghost.
Pray until you speak in tongues — let the Holy Ghost take you
captive. The Word of God guarantees, when the Holy Spirit comes
upon you, **YOU SHALL RECEIVE POWER**.

Chapter Seven

YOU'VE GOT WORK TO DO!

God has placed great value in you. When He sent His Son Jesus to the cross, He had a great redemption plan in mind. Not only would He forgive your sins, but He would clean you up, too! God desired to put a new heart in you and make you a brand new person. He desired that you would learn His ways and become more like Him every day. Ultimately, He is longing to see you in Heaven some day soon where you will live forever with Him.

His redemption plan was very thorough. He was able, through the death and resurrection of Jesus, to turn you completely around. Now, instead of living for the devil, you are living for Jesus — and you will bring others to Heaven with you.

I never cease to be amazed at how wonderful God is. Recently I met some of my old high school buddies. We were at our 50th high school reunion. When some of my buddies asked what I was doing, I told them that I have been preaching the Gospel of Jesus Christ for over 50 years.

Their reaction was one of shock: "YOU, SHAMMY? You were the worst one of the bunch!"

They weren't just kidding. I was the worst. But, oh, how grateful I am to God. He took the worst one of the bunch, saved me and so radically changed me that I am able to lead others to Jesus. God doesn't choose you because you are good or smart — He chooses you because you have a great job to do.

This is what Jesus told His disciples:

"Go therefore and make disciples of all the nations, baptizing them in the name of the Father and of the Son and of the Holy Spirit,

"teaching them to observe all things that I have commanded you; and lo, I am with you always, even to the end of the age."
(Matthew 28:19,20)

God surely knows how to get a good return on His investment! He will use everything He has taught you to bring even more people to Heaven.

Your job description is easy. As you learn about Jesus, you teach others what you have learned. You won't have to worry about what you will say — He said He would **always** be with you. Earlier in the Bible He gave His disciples a similar promise:

"...do not worry about how or what you should speak. For it will be given to you in that hour what you should speak."
(Matthew 10:19)

You can believe that God never intended for you to sit still. He wants you to be active for Him. Some people are good at preaching; others can sing well. Some love to cook and clean — they can visit the sick or elderly and be a real help to them. Many love working with children or young people. You know that there will never be a shortage of people who need Jesus.

Jesus told His disciples they were chosen to be active for Him. He referred to their work as "bearing fruit."

> *"You did not choose Me, but I chose you and appointed you that you should go and bear fruit, and that your fruit should remain, that whatever you ask the Father in My name He may give you."*
> (John 15:16)

God will begin to speak to your heart about how you can be busy for Him. He will use all of your gifts and talents to win others to Christ, if you allow Him.

Jesus also told His disciples something very important. If they were to bear fruit — and keep doing His work — they would need spiritual strength.

> *"I am the true vine, and My Father is the vinedresser...*
>
> *"Abide in Me, and I in you. As the branch cannot bear fruit of itself, unless it abides in the vine, neither can you, unless you abide in Me."*
> (John 15:1,4)

All the lessons you learn as you grow up in Jesus will help you bear fruit in the future. When you pray every day, you are abiding in Jesus. As you read the Bible daily, you are abiding in Jesus. Not only are you learning more facts, but you are learning to allow Jesus to govern your life. This is very important when you start working for Him. You must do exactly as He instructs you.

I hope you are excited about serving Jesus. There is no

greater privilege — and no greater wonder. What a joy it is to think the great God of the universe can use someone like me in His master plan! You are chosen for a reason. Get busy — you've got work to do.

And remember, you are **one in a million!**

Chapter Eight

YOU WILL MAKE IT!

I have given you quite a bit to digest and to put into practice; but of this one thing I am certain — **YOU WILL MAKE IT!** If you are careful to do all that you have been instructed to do, God will see to it that you succeed as a Christian.

Remember the instructions you have received:

1.   Read your Bible every day.

2.   Pray and worship God daily.

3.   Regularly ask God to forgive you of your sins and to help you grow in your faith walk.

4.   Find a church home and be active in it.

5.   Ask God to baptize you with the Holy Ghost until

you speak in tongues. Then pray in tongues every day.

6.   Tell others about Jesus. Become a soul winner.

I am so happy you have decided to follow Jesus. In a few months or years, I believe you will be writing to me telling me of all the miracles God is performing in your life. You will be telling me about family members you have brought to Jesus. What an exciting walk of faith you have begun!

Remember that Sister Schambach and I, along with my entire ministry team, are praying for you often. We believe in you. You are God's child. You are family. **YOU ARE ONE IN A MILLION.**

OTHER HELPFUL BOOKS BY R. W. SCHAMBACH
AND POWER PUBLICATIONS

The Power of Faith for Today's Christian

When You Wonder "Why?"

Power Struggle - *Faith for Difficult Relationships*

Triumphant Faith

Tell, Teach and Train (Donna Schambach)

The Miracle Manual - *An Evangelism and Prayer Handbook*

WHEN YOU NEED PRAYER

Call the Power Phone

Every day of the week, 24 hours a day, a dedicated, faith-filled, Bible-believing Prayer Partner is ready to talk with you and pray about your needs. When you need prayer, call:

(903) 894-6141